A Merry-Mouse Book of Months

A
MERRY-
MOUSE
BOOK

Doubleday & Company, Inc.
Garden City, New York

A Merry-Mouse
Book of Months

by Priscilla Hillman

Library of Congress Cataloging in Publication Data
Hillman, Priscilla.
A Merry-Mouse Book of Months.
SUMMARY:
Brief poems introduce the months of the year.
1. Months—Juvenile poetry. [1. Months—Poetry]
I. Title.
PS3558.I453M4   811′.5′4

Library of Congress Catalog Card Number 79—8021
ISBN: 0—385—15594—8 Trade
ISBN: 0—385—15595—6 Prebound

9 8 7 6 5 4 3 2

To my son, Glenn

January starts the year
With softly falling snow.
I wonder if our "snowmouse"
Can feel the cold wind blow.

February means it's time
To send out Valentines.
I've made you one all by myself.
I hope you will be mine.

March brings cold and blustery days
With promises of spring.
I wish my kite would fly as high
As a robin on the wing.

April is the rainy month
With gentle springtime showers.
So remember your umbrella
When you go out picking flowers.

May is a month of blossoms
Nodding in the air.
Did you think a tulip
Could be a mouse's chair?

June is a time of buzzing bees.
The air is warm and bright.
We whisper "hi" to a butterfly
And a firefly says, "Good night."

July is the time to play outside.
We're having so much fun,
Swinging through the grasses
Under the summer sun.

August brings hot and lazy days
For lying in the shade.
We like to pack a basket
For a picnic in the glade.

September ends the summer days.
It's back to school once more.
Here's an apple for our teacher.
Oops! We've only left the core.

October is the golden month,
The month of Halloween.
Look! We're climbing the biggest pumpkin
That we have ever seen.

November brings in colder days
For winter's almost here.
We gather berries, nuts, and corn.
It's harvest time of year.

December brings us Christmas
With jingle bells and joy.
And Santa Mouse will visit soon
And leave a Christmas toy.

*Now these mice know every month
In winter, summer, spring, and fall.
They can say all twelve of them—
Do you know them all?*

Calendar

19 2
26 27 2

Priscilla Hillman is a self-taught artist who has been interested in drawing ever since she was a child and spent many hours sketching with her twin sister, Greta. On the advice of a high school art teacher, Ms. Hillman did not attend an art school. Instead, she studied botany at the University of Rhode Island and subsequently worked for two years at the U. S. Oceanographic Office in Maryland.

Shortly after she was married, however, Ms. Hillman resumed her interest and self-education in art. For several years she has painted and designed artwork for greeting cards, gift wrap, and stationery, but she has only recently begun to write and illustrate her own books.

The artist lives in New York State with her husband, Norm, and their ten-year-old son, Glenn. Besides painting and writing verse, Ms. Hillman's interests include listening to classical music and observing nature, especially birds.